Sunfire

Sunfire

A Collection of Poems

James A. Ciletti

TERRA PUBLICATIONS

TERRA PUBLICATIONS

Copyright 2006 James A. Ciletti

Published 2006 by Terra Publications, a division of Odyssey Books,
545 Collyer Street, Longmont, CO 80501

Printed in Boulder, Colorado by Johnson Printing. All rights reserved. Except as
permitted under the United States Copyright Act, no part of this publication may
be reproduced or distributed in any form or by any means, or stored in a database
or retrieval system, without prior written permission from the publisher, unless
otherwise indicated.

ISBN 0-9768655-1-3

1 2 3 4 5 6 7 8 9 10

Acknowledgments

The author acknowledges the periodicals that first published some of these poems, including *Plainsong, The Silver Lode, The Frank Waters Newsletter, Crested Butte Pilot, Rocky Mountain Creative Arts Journal, The Washington Reporter, Pilgrimage, Cadence, Italian Americana, Heartlodge,* and *Poetry on the Lake.*

Table of Contents

Introduction   1

Sunfire   3

Sound the Trumpets

Chopping Firewood   7
Ode to a Ripe Plum   8
Holding Hands, a Lover's Grounding   9
I Know a Man Half Deaf   10
Dearest Mary   12
A Junkyard Must Be Heaven   14
Mr. Fee's Doctoral Thesis   15
Daughter in My Arms   16
Daffodils   17
Standing in the Kitchen   18
Joy to You Today   20
Button My Lip   22
Tomato Love   24
Lady   25
Breathe into Your Dreams   28
We Walked a Yellow Balloon   30

When the Poet Looks in the Mirror

Sleepless, Middle of the Night, Journal Notes   33
Out the Windows   35
When a Poem Wears Muddy Boots   36
Word Magic   40
The Poet's Lament   41
Shopping at the Hardware Store   42

I Milk the Sky and the Earth

That Woodpecker   45
Wooden Fence Post   46
Geography 101   47
Quiet of a Spring Morning   50
Arizona Suaro   51
Colorado Prairie with the Best of Miles Davis   52
Doing Nothing   54
Coming into Indian Presence   55
I Want to Hold Still in the Mountains   56
Watching the Hawk Above the Desert   57
Two Haiku   59
Morning Doves   60

Tomatoes and Eggplants Ripen at Night

Redeeming Snowflakes   63
Grandmother's Bread Song   64
Sunday Dinner 1956   65
Uncle Joe's Onions   68
Chew Mail Pouch   69
Father O'Malley Meets Barbarella at Her Pinball Machine   72
House Blessings   74
Grandmother, Grandfather   75
Recipes from Italy   76
Italian Omelets   78

Beware! The Drums of War

Holy Faith, White Crosses   81
The Wednesday Before Easter   83
Black Crows in a Red Sunrise   84
At 6 a.m. This Snowy Daylight Dawning   87
Kent 4, May 4, 1970   88

The Strong Basket Holds Everything

Spinning with Galileo   93
Two More Haiku   94
Getting the Newspaper from the Lawn   95
Dreaming in Fish Breath   96
Gorillas in the Mist at the YMCA   97
Tangerine   98
Ah! The Last Two Haiku   99
In Barney's Diner   100
Peachy   102
New Snow, Jack   103
Always Look Twice   104
When I Die   105
Transparent as the Grass   107
In the Sunfire   109

Introduction

How easily, almost thoughtlessly, we arise at the crack of dawn, stretch open our sleepy eyes, massage our groggy face, rub a hand through our hair and brush our teeth. We dress, check the mirror to see if our tie is straight or if our skirt's the right length.

Do my shoes match?

And what about shaving?

Putting on eyeliner?

Without a mirror? Forget it.

Faced with the face of ourselves, we know what to do, what to fix or leave alone. Faced with the face of ourselves, we know how to make our private face public to enter the world.

So too with thinking and writing. Without reflection in words, what a smear of red lipstick our thoughts will be; without verbal investigation the bleeding cuts in our ideas; and so too, the darkness in our hearts, without words to express and know our feelings.

When we use words to express our core emotions and thoughts we are expressing our core identity. Want to know who you are? Walk into the garden of yourself? Look at the reflection of yourself in the mirrors of your words.

Just as we need a mirror to see our spine, the back of our head, neck, etc., we need the mirror of language to face the face of our thoughts. Our words show us where the tie of our opinion needs straightened; the lipstick of our politeness needs daubed; facing the face of our thoughts and fears and joys, values, dreams and prayers, we can see who we are, inside.

Thus, our words, written in thoughtful reflection, can mirror back to us an emotional knowledge from the deepest vaults of our self, our core identity, and our soul. Our words mirror our heart. For me, the ultimate joy of poetry, and all of art, occurs when our creativity reflects and celebrates the human heart.

Sunfire

In blazing sunfire
Shadowless, we stand naked
Born again in light.

Sound the Trumpets

Chopping Firewood

I love splitting wood on winter days when
air holds my face with cold hands
my mouth breathes out white sky
warm sunlight soothes my bruised bones.

I love splitting wood on winter days
when I roll these barreled stumps
to a certain distance before me,
separate my feet, and dig in my heels.

Eyeing the center ring
I raise this ax above my head,
brace it as all the ropes and
wires in my arms and back
wind and coil to strike down
this ax
again and again and again
like a fan blade wild in sunlight
until the pine crackles open
and smells clean enough to bite.

With a hand on each half
I open the log and
feel the pine
fly up into my face in flames.

Ode to a Ripe Plum

There is but one way to celebrate a plump
Ripe plum
Polish it on your shirtsleeve,
See your face in its silvery black shine then
Open wide, lock your lips on the skin,
Sink your teeth into the sensuous center
Suck in the flesh, slurp up the juices.

Ah! The purple of it all.

Swirl your tongue around the fleshy fruit
Sip succulent sugary sap
Ssssssslllllllpp.
Slobber if you must but, oh,
Taste, sensate, celebrate the
Plum's plump purple passion until
You quiver shiver scintillate with the
Small sour pithy particle palpitating at
Your tongue's tip and that last tart bite
Puckers your mouth with plump plum-ish delight.

Plums. Pllumms.
PPPPlluuuuummmmmmmms.
Oh, I love plums.
I love *ripe* plums.
My kingdom for a plum.
Yes!
There is but one way
To celebrate plump plum ripeness
In your mouth. Aaaaaah!
The purple of it all.

Holding Hands, My Lover's Grounding

With your voice trembling, you said,
"Please hold my hand."
I thought we were going to do
something as mundane and
practical as holding hands, then stare out
the window at the pink granite mountains.

Even though we shared friends, books, coffee,
we were but two somebodies who could
easily be confused, like miners with dim candles,
searching for gold in worked-out mines.

Touching, slipping fingers to fingers we left
scripted conventions behind, old maps crumbled.
We dug deeper, pressed fingers tightly,
drilling open fresh ores; our cracked vanity,
the schist of fool's gold, crumbled.

My darling, our touching made us perfect
the vibrations in our tectonic plates
shifted to a flow in the veins through
the hardened lava with new harmonics,
barely visible in our pulsing temples,
neck, drum beating wrists, fingertips, lips
a mother lode dreamed of but never expected.

We were going to be something ordinary, the
usual glitter of fool's gold. Now, 14 years later,
dearest lady, we live together in our loving grace,
fingers to fingers, palms to palms, a great treasure
from the flinty spark of your words,
"I need grounded. Please hold my hand."

I Know a Man Half Deaf

I know a man with ears half deaf and eyes half blind, who each day awakens to the call of his house-mate and a breakfast of her biscuits and gravy, a garage full of tools, and his cars and trucks. Mr. Fee lives across the alley from me and his garage has one of every hand tool known to man and power ones too.

I saw this man, with my own two eyes, take an old beat up pickup truck with rear tandem wheels, and remove the bed, rebuild the engine, get a junkyard dump-truck box, figure and draw and re-draw, design and weld together the frame and even build, assemble and attach the hydraulics, until he had a dump truck. Which he painted black and brown and red and I took a photo of him standing proud, grinning, beside it.

When he stood back and admired his work, he said he never "gradgeated" high school because of a wreck. When Mr. Fee, at the age of 16, "had bought myself an old 32 Ford and shined it all up and got 'er running and then loaned it to a friend. The friend wrecked the Ford into a new Buick and the friend then left town."

This man, then a boy of 16 heard his father say, "You'll have to quit school son, that car he used was yours and you'll have to pay to fix that Buick."

"And so I did and got a job in a gas station on East Platte and paid off the repairs of that new Buick and then learned car mechanics."

Even though he has no degree on paper, he is a professor of smooth-running valves, the logic of carburetors, and the seams of a beautiful weld. Mr. Fee has a bachelor's degree in scraped knuckles and prized swear words, a master's degree in nuts and bolts and a doctorate in car repairs and the philosophy of combustible engines.

Mr. Fee, with a face of a polished fender, is pushing 75. Yes, he wears hearing aids yet can hear a car purr softer'n a kitten.

Forgets his glasses and squints to read directions and has stubby scarred fingers, a car mechanic's knuckles and hands with scars on scars. If you bring something to him to fix, he'll never say he can do it, but will look you right in the eye and say, "We'll give 'er a try." And you come back next day and sure enough, he's welded that paper-thin steel and got your handle back on your son's little red wagon.

I nearly caused a divorce once because I said to my wife, "Honey, if we plane-wreck on a stranded island and it comes down to a toss up between you and Mr. Fee, I'd rather have Mr. Fee cause he'd surely fix whatever I need to get me home."

Mr. Fee loves oatmeal cookies, smiles through old teeth, constantly wears a war paint of grease smears, and despite his lack of that high school diploma, he's a master in the logic of timing gears, fuel pumps, shock absorbers, vacuum hoses and a philosopher of drive shafts and gear ratios, and all so wise in the way of chugging carburations. Lacking medical credentials he can do CPR on a car and yes, when pressed to perform, Mr. Fee probably can mend a broken heart or weld the crack of dawn.

Dearest Mary,

At 6:30 this morning, I started to write a summer poem for you. I had the very best of intentions and if I were a fine painter I'd have started with our bedroom, morning light through the blinds onto the white sheets covering all of you except one bare leg, beautiful skin, angled out, and your face, haloed with dark hair, so soft in the morning light.

But such a scene eludes my painting skills.

I took my notebook, put a pen in my pocket, and headed for the patio. But passing through the kitchen I stopped to make a pot of coffee. Then, outside I had to drag the sprinkler and hose to the front yard, make sure the chug-chug spitz-spitz spits of spray hit the dry spots, and then I came to the patio to write a poem. I opened my notebook to a page of clean white paper and then inhaled the aroma of coffee.

In the kitchen, I poured my coffee. In my mind's eye I saw you roll so that your face looked up at me and you smiled.

Coffee in hand I returned to the patio.

At the table, notebook before me, pen in hand, I looked out to the garden. I wanted to see the zucchini blossoms we'll make with eggs for breakfast. Of course I had to inspect the green tomatoes. I had to calculate the days and nights until they burst ripe red in your mouth. I will kiss you then.

I walked barefoot in the wet grass. The cool lush green rush of a summery chill tickled my feet, goose-bumped my legs. Is this the same when I kiss your neck?

Finally I was ready to write. But first I had to reposition the spitting sprinkler, and I needed more coffee, that aroma of Jakarta. Out the kitchen window I watched a red-throated finch pecking the first of the dry sunflowers for seeds. I had to wait for him to finish, else opening the screen door might shoo him away.

Out on the patio, the distant drone of a single-engine airplane. Closer, the clash of cars shushing up Union Boulevard set me off, and the shriek of the very close flicker and right beside me the gurgle-urgle of the water fountain girl pouring water, ceaselessly, gurgle gurgle, and closer yet, the silence of my hand's shadow gliding across this page. Yes, Mary, I awoke with the best of intentions, to write a poem for you.

By now, both of your bare legs are angled out from the milky sheets. The bees are working in the sunflowers, tomatoes, and zucchini blossoms. The green beans need picked, and I'm about to go inside with an empty coffee cup.

In the bedroom, I will awaken you with my kisses.

A Junkyard Must Be Heaven

For Jimmy, my buddy on trips to the recycling yard

A junkyard must be heaven
When you're five and a half
In your father's big red truck,
Squidging your face against the window,
Bulging your eyes to watch the big crane
Lift whole car bodies into the blue sky.
And the noise of it all makes you say,
"It scares my ears, but it's fun."

The joy of it all
When you're five and a half
And can hold tight to your father
As he lifts you to touch the yellow crane
And your tongue tastes the happy air.

The glory of it all
In the scale room, where father
Takes his junking money and buys
A cola of your own, and his friends ask,
"Who's your big helper today?"
And the pride of it all as father
Pays a quarter to you as well.

Yes, a junkyard must be heaven
When you're five and a half
Going on forever,
With a quarter and a cola,
Falling asleep against your father,
Dreaming, of returning again and again
To the heaven of the junkyard.

Mr. Fee's Doctoral Thesis

I was over at Mr. Fee's today when
he was working on that Ford again. Shoulda seen 'im.
You know, he took out the whole steering column,
pulled out the ignition wiring and deft as a surgeon
spliced, fixed and replaced it all.

Shoulda seen 'im, old Mr. Fee
sitting in that big white Ford truck,
his grey hair, his back straight, mind ticking,
and ready to turn the key for the first time
and that engine RRRRRRRR-ed and cranked right up
and he hit the gas pedal and blew out the puffy blue smoke
until the exhaust was clear. Now he's just sitting there,
looking out over the steering wheel, glazed eyed,
and you can see his inner ear listening to
the engine with each push of the gas pedal,
his inner ear an invisible stethoscope, picking out
each tick-beat of the V-8 engine piston strokes,
looking straight ahead through infinite caculations,
sounding out for a miss, a valve tick, a testing push on the gas,
a hard rev of the engine, a few more revs REVS,
he tilts his head, listens one last time,
face bearded with grease, he looks out at me
shuts off the engine and says,
"I think we got 'er now." Shoulda seen him,
his smile as wide as a chrome bumper.

Daughter in My Arms
A lullaby for Laura

Child in my arms, crying,
Your voice startles my skin,
Awakens my body. Holding you
I hold myself once, crying.

I press you close to my face,
Close as light on buttercups.
Ashes in my bones sing for you,
Sing quiet as dreams sleeping.
Sleeping.
Sleep, my sweet daughter.
Spinning like a top into tomorrow
Your face lights up this room;
Your breathing stirs stars of dust
Descending on us, sleep, sleep.

Sleeping,
Your eyes dream like small birds
Watching moon surprise the night.
Daughter in my arms, dreaming,
I kiss your light face, sleeping.

Daffodils

Ten yellow daffodils trumpet up and
out of the vase. Six petals
collar each yellow trumpet
nature's innocence incenses my eyes with????
What? What?
Suddenly, I have nothing to say about
ten yellow daffodils circling periscope trumpets
up from the white vase.

Each daffodil's outer circle,
so translucent, a halo of light,
weaves in and out, creating crinkled
open lips to the mouth of the yellow trumpet.

I have nothing to say about
six petals collaring each curly edged trumpet.
Nothing to hide about six pollen petals
hugging the stamen deep inside the trumpet.

And if you see these ten yellow daffodils
obedient unto themselves, guilty of no original or
other sin, gracing the table with a yellow so delicious
you want to lick it, would you demand their confession
for having group sex? Require a penance
for their giving to you this communion?

Standing in the Kitchen

I am the one standing at the kitchen window
to spy on the green shoots of garlic
in those neat rows surrounded by snow.

I am the one watching the sparrow
hunt and peck for seeds under
the snow-covered patio table.

I am the one who hears the trees sigh
under the weight of a spring snow.
Yes, I am the one,
I am the one planting
geranium cuttings at the windowsill and
spritzing the volunteer marigold seedlings.

I am the one who just sipped coffee
and felt the hammer head of blunt pain
ache and throb in my broken right arm.

I am the one who breathes, alive.
who will cook dinner
who lives patiently
and watches an endless flow of water
trickling from the maiden's vase in the bird bath.
I am the one standing at the kitchen window,
to watch you tip-toe across the snow-wet lawn.

Do you see the watering can
capsized by the onion bed,
the cap of snow on the flower pot,
the tree shadows' blue?

I am the one watching you
climbing up the steps, holding the blue railing,
entering our shuddering door and
walking over to this notebook and
reading that you are the one
standing in the kitchen with me.

Joy to You Today

I sing.
Sing to celebrate this glorious day.
As Mary sleeps, her eyelashes flutter
shuddering movie pictures,
what dreams she feels I cannot guess.
Oh, Mary! I loved you before you were born.

Now I kiss your ears to see you awaken
to this song of a new day as you roll over
and your eyes open bright and we say together,
"Good morning."

I did not know how much I loved the feminine in you
until I saw you at the mirror, angling your head
and your neck, the neck I love to kiss,
and without looking you felt by finger touch, and
instinctively locked into place that gold loop earring.

I did not know how much I loved the feminine in you
until I saw your arms and hands come together
as the shower pelted your face and head
and then you wiped back your hair
stepped out of the shower and I could smell
the lemons and summer-ripe tomatoes and
sweet basil in the aroma of your skin.

I did not know how much I loved
the constellation of freckles on your back
until I dried the beads of water on your shoulders.

When you turn into the first light of dawn
I know now how much I love you
and
as I see that oval of light, your face,
and
as the earth turns sunward
I know we will kiss in the sunfire.

Button My Lip

Viewing "A Field of Buttons," a painting by Tom Rogers

That creamy yellow one, I'm sure came from
my lover's blouse, she yanked it open to expose the
tops of her breasts, puckered the button between her lips,
taunted me to bite it from her with my teeth.
And so I, well, later —

Oh! That slippery emerald green button washed ashore
in Positano, Italy, the day the squid fisherman drowned
while trying to save his boat in the storm.

If only Lee Harvey Oswald had had a shirt that
took too long to button
too long to button.

You know that fire-headed dancer,
she popped the pink buttons,
angrily ripped off and threw her costume at
the choreographer, who was sleeping with the male lead.

Buttons. Who has the shirt that the silver one graced?
Who buttoned up Napoleon?
Who unbuttons you?

Don't be fooled by the lavender one, if you slip
through the holes you'll be smelling the sulphurous
breath of the devil and want to escape into
that fetal pose inside the Virgin Mary.

What you don't smell in these buttons are the
peaches we stole from the roadside tree
in Yakima, Washington.

But, oh! How sweet the aroma, delicious the taste,
my ears swelling in revelry when I press my head
to the button-less bosom of my lover and
listen to the radio in her chest, all night long.

Tomato Love

One skin-tight bite
of this sweet tarty tomato
cancels all dominion of the self.

Tasting the flesh in this flesh
one easily becomes translucent.
criss-crossing the tomato heart,
brigades of sensations sensate my mouth.

So what's this shake-out between
eating tomatoes and making love?
This skin blushing red to a simple touch,
this full fleshy feeling plump in the hand,
aroma divine of the love apple from the vine,
the skin kissable above or below the nipple or navel?

For what's a kiss on the cheek, or luscious red lips,
but the flesh of a tomato ripe in the mouth.
Ah! To live where tomatoes ripen every day!
Every hour! Now! Taste the tarty tomato.

Lady

1.
Your hands embarrass the sun
Radiating in a crow's feather,
And you want to wear gloves!?

Your hands ripen peaches
And make the rain talk to itself;
When you cup your hands over my ears
I hear the sea singing.
And you want to wear gloves!

Then wear these gloves made
With the first finger from sunlight combed
From your colt's mane;
The second from the honey I've gathered
From your golden breasts;
The third from behind your ears
The scent of freshly plowed earth;
The fourth finger is the face of
Morning on your cheekbones.

The thumb?
Easy. . .
I simply sift the moonlight
Ripening in your hair
And mix it with the wheat fields
Shining on your knees.

2.
First you came like the wind in
A child's hand and I stood
With a child's mouth open.
Then you came like feathers falling
Between snowflakes and I stood
With a tree's arms reaching.

Next, you zeroed in like night bombers
And I knelt in terror, my ribs open,
Sending up searchlights.

Now you don't even knock.

I turn around in the marketplace
And there's your hand in the apples.
I walk the dark streets and you follow
Disguised as winter wind blowing
Night against my neck.
I fall asleep and dream of you pulling on
Your long white boots.
I wash, reach for a towel,
And your hands dry my face.

Your hands with the fragrance of almonds,
Your fingers, the ribs of a ship.
Your presence, like eagle tracks
That neither come nor go.

3.
I marvel at the magic and
Mystery of your entrance into
My flesh and bones.
How sweet your presence.

4.
All birds land. But you never land.
All streams and rivers pour down and out
Until they lie still and deep in oceans.
But you ebb and flow, ebb and flow, in my blood.

5.
You are not here.
Then why, for the last ten minutes,
Have I been brushing your hair?
Jesus walked on water.
Our spacemen jumped into the moon's eyes.
You dance around these rooms inside of me
And I hear your hands, clapping.

6.
I want no name for this.
No words to fence you in.
I will never hear your same voice twice.
No matter how many lights I shine
I will never search nor discover
All that is in your rooms.
This is the miracle I love.
Like hiking up the mountains,
I keep moving with the pull of the path
To discover what is beyond the trees,
Or around the bend in your elbow.

Breathe into Your Dreams
To an emergency helicopter flight nurse

1.
This woman in white,
Flying over mountains, with bloody hands,
Teaching firemen to breathe for babies
Saving lives like a Jesus
Wants to open a farmer's feed store with
A room for stoneware pottery.

As she sits for mid-morning coffee with
A clay cup cradled in her hands
Her head tilts over heart. She
Listens to something so close as
To be inside of her.

2.
Woman in white, what sweet milk you are
Hands cut from bailing wire,
Knees bruised from chasing horses at midnight,
Your fingers pumping plasma into a dying man.

3.
Woman in white, take this dream stillborn and
Place your lips over its mouth and
Breathe until this new brain fires with hot blood and
Breathe and breathe until
These new lungs scream and breathe,
Breathe! Until these new eyes open
And your sweat beads into tight kernels

And breathe and breathe as grains bulge in
Fat sacks, and moonlight swells in your veins.
Breathe until your face glows in daylight and
Your white uniform splits up the middle and
Your heart flies out as you hover there with
Your heels caked with earth and light and you
Breathe.

4.
Breathe into your dreams until
You see your hand among the oats,
Flakes of wheat chaff in your chestnut hair
And breathe and breathe until
Your body bends to buck a bale of hay
And breathe and breathe
With the farmers and ranchers and their animal needs;
Breathe with the rising sun.
As your key unlocks the door
As you breathe
And your breathing and quiet feet stir ·
Dust into daylight.

5.
Woman in blue,
Your breathing swells the small rooms
And you breathe and breathe and blow
Steam off mid-morning coffee;
Breathe as you look at the stoneware pottery,
Breathe and breathe into your dreams as you listen,
Woman in bib overalls, listen
To all that is close and inside of you.

We Walked a Yellow Balloon
For Josine

Walking a yellow balloon
High as our shoulder
String tight in our hand
We pretended to limp.

Our yellow balloon limped.
We stuttered, the balloon stuttered.
We three laughed up the L-train stairs.
Sitting on a green bench
We waited for a green train.
Our yellow balloon touched
Against your hair
Sparked
Bounced over to me then
Back to you.

On the train we sat and talked,
Rode north to Loyola Station,
Our balloon
Tight on a string
Tight in our hand
Pointed south
Hovering, inches behind our head.

When the Poet Looks in the Mirror

Sleepless, Middle of the Night, Journal Notes

After tossing in sleeplessness I sit by the window. In 2 a.m. darkness I scribble here in my journal. Yellow sodium vapor street lights cast an eerie and lemony-sour light down to the trees, pavement, the yard. Across the street in our neighbor's driveway, his Chevy truck, a for sale sign in the window, the dual headlights, rimmed with chrome, stare out towards Kansas, Cincinnati, Virginia Beach, to the splashing moon-lit waves of the Atlantic.

Aiming directly at me, coming up Uintah Street, the hot white bright lights of a moving car. Who is in the car, where are they going? To work at the hospital? To score a drug deal? To a sleeping spouse?

What truck's cruising eastward through Missouri? Is the driver chewing gum, or lip puffed with snuff, maybe listening to Johnny Cash? Thinking about a stop for pie and coffee? Flirting with the waitress?

What ship with a triangle string of lights is passing through the Strait of Juan de Fuca, heading towards Seattle with a cargo of "American toys" made in China?

What child in the Sudan is scratching her empty tummy? The eye sockets weep even after death. The nails from Christ's cross have rusted into the earth. Even the flies are dying of starvation.

Another car with blazing lights passes.

Are lovers strolling the beach in Monte Carlo? Is a bus skidding over a cliff in Columbia? In Bari, Italy, the fishermen are docking their blue and yellow boats, sniffling cold noses and eager for a cappuccino.

Tall grain elevators in Nebraska stand speechless, unable to read the New York Times.

This night in Colorado Springs, steam clouds billow up from the Martin Drake power plant. The truck driver changes channels. But the catfish in the Mississippi know your name. Why else would you get up in the middle of the night to hear their stories?

Sleepless? Take two poems, drink lots of imagery, and go to sleep.

Out the Windows

Out the front window, in Acacia Park
the jubilant jumping kiddies and diapered babies
shrieking and frolicking in Uncle Wilbur's fountain?
Or out the back window down to the alley?
You tell me, where is the poem? The rap?
The first-prize painting?

In the scraped knuckles and calloused hands
of the trash men hefting that bin?
In the thumping pumping hearts
of the vigilant mothers attending their children?
In the trained eyes of the draftsman who
designed the grid for the model for
the forged steel manhole cover?

You tell me. What do you want the poem to be?

The right brain blood vessels of the musician
who created the circus-like music inspiring
the leaps and laughter of the children?
Perhaps the precise craftsmanship
of the masons who laid the fountain tiles?
The artist who painted them.
The scientist who developed the clay formula.
Look at their smiles, look at their sweat.
You tell me.

When a Poem Wears Muddy Boots

A true poem stomps in wearing boots caked with
Mud from planting garlic, throbs with a splinter
Under its fingernail, and wakes in the middle
Of the night with leg cramps and dreams of flying.

A true poem drips with the red of sunfire in the mist,
At that magical moment when, facing the sunrise,
That split second, when no one can kill anyone.

The cleavage of a true poem sprouts
Zucchini blossoms, cooks broccoli soup with
Cream and butter and serves crusty warm bread.

Sometimes a true poem yanks a fishhook through
Your eyelids, gives you bloodshot traffic lights for eyes.
Yes. The really true poem cheers for Afghan girls
Going back to school; it cries for their mothers beaten
In the streets; its fingertips bleed with frostbite from the
Snow of Sarajevo, red with blood of
Sled-riding children dismembered by man-made bombs.

Beware of the fish swimming between your legs.
Beware of this poem.
Beware of the fox sitting on the lawn.
Beware! The morning dove coos; your breasts are
Warm from sleeping on them. Watch out! Beware!

A true poem is a warrior with a shield of paper, and
Wears a hunting vest with pens, pencils, and
Crayons filling bullet tubes. A true poem salutes you,

Smells flowers, kisses babies, then takes off its boots
Before entering the house and making love with you.

If this poem be true its bare feet
Are caked with mud and blood from
Earth and man-kind and children-kind and a
Million kernels of red rice falling from its eyes and
Pumpkin flowers blossoming out of its mouth.

This poem kneels to kiss the earth and
Sunfire on your lips.
When the poem is true the words sneak out at night to
Swirl with moths around the street light. At the
Crack of dawn the poem staggers home with
Wrinkled wings, a swollen face, and black eyes.

Sometimes a poem deserves a speeding ticket
For driving too slowly; other times a fine for driving
Faster than the speed of life.
Now the traffic light turns red.
Yet, the poem sips coffee, awaits sunrise. The dark
Blue sky clings to silver vest buttons of night.

Sometimes the true poem goes to bed hungry,
Growls, and dreams with owls and children, then
Shivers in the cold. Even in the chilly dark
This poem sees its own breath.

The scent of rosemary chicken fills the kitchen. Fresh
Bread rises in the oven, and if you walk away hungry.
Don't blame this poem. There's enough chicken and
Bread for everyone.

This poem hears babies sleeping with chirping
Crickets on the plains of Africa. So this poem holds

Hands with widowers in Chiapas, and sings a requiem for
All the sailors and soldiers at the bottom of the sea.
Hey! We cannot cry forever.
Sooner or later we throw down our tears, pick up
Our shovels, and spade the garden until
The "plow down sillion" shines and
We set aside the wee "Mousie's" nest.

At the crack of dawn, we cannot shoot anyone.
All trees are black, but white in our mind. All the
Streetlights shine on dark waters. At the crack of dawn,
The pigeons are black on electric lines, and
Our toast and coffee pass through wires in their feet.

Yes, the poet is a high-wire walker. Like the
Pigeons on the electric wires, the poet too, is an
Electrician. With both hands he or she picks up
The hot wires and sparks them together and on any day
Or night you can see the poet
Glowing in the dark, frazzled in the light.

Sometimes the poet is a heart surgeon. But don't expect
This poem to kiss your breasts nor make you swoon.
Expect, yes, demand that the poem slip out of its
Skin and bones, tap you on the shoulder, make you
Turn around and place your hands on hot wires,
Zap you, and then laugh at you when you cry.
Yes, a good poem slaps your face and says,
"Snap out of it!" And you say,
"Thank you! Do that again."

Let's face it, a good poem anoints you
With your own blood. Makes you kneel down and
Confess your sins as the hot wires pass
Through your fingertips to God.

Beware.
Beware of poems in white shirts and professorial robes,
that way madness lies, helium-filled ideas,
knocked free of mud, rising so high they burst.
Beware even more of what drips from
The colander of your brain.

By now you know the really good poems
The ones you can pick up, shine 'em red
On your sleeve, bite into them,
Crunch your teeth into the white pulp,
Feel the juices running down your chin.

Above all, remember, the best poems don't give you gas.
The best poems wear muddy boots, smell of garlic,
Taste like kisses and smack you with ecstasy.

Note: "Sheer plod makes plough down sillion/Shine" is from "The Windhover
by Gerard Manley Hopkins

"Mousie" is from "To a Mouse" by Robert Burns

Word Magic

If this poem were pottery
it would hold new wine,
or if a dancer's legs
these words would jump and jive.

If this poem were a stream
you could stick your hand
into this page and pull up
sparkling fresh water to your lips.

If this poem were my father
it would walk bowlegged
and praise itself for saving
five cents on day-old bread.

If this poem were the night sky
you'd feel the stars
sink their teeth into
the back of your head.

But since this poem doesn't hold new wine,
doesn't jump and jive,
and you can't get fresh water here,
nor see my bowlegged father,
I guess the best thing to do
is to reach into the back of your head
and put the stars back into the sky.

This Poet's Lament

If I could sing like Pavarotti
My bones would glow in the dark.
But I sing more like clods of dirt.
If I could dance like Juliet
My eyes would see themselves.
But I dance like tree stumps
And scales have covered my eyes
For many years.

If I could love as sure as the sun
My heart would stop screaming.
But I love like a river
Changing course on the hour.
Perhaps tonight I should sit on the roof
And gargle with moonlight,
Beg the wind to rip off my clothes,
Invite the morning sunfire to burn holes
Into my heart.

Shopping at the Hardware Store

A teacher of modern literature complained to me that
Contemporary poetry "has too many dirty words."
So I said to her: "I'm fixing the pipeline to my hot
Water heater. To finish the job I went to the hardware
Store for pipe nipples and a street L with male threads at
One end and female threads at the other."

The teacher blushed. I continued.

"Sometimes threads are stripped, so I tested them. When I
Screwed the male end into the female threads I noticed
Burrs inside the pipe. So I borrowed the hardware store's
Bastard file to ream out the steel filings. Then I smoothly,
Tightly, screwed the pipes together."

Her face reddened.
"Next, I purchased a water cock."
Quickly, she looked away, down at her feet.

"Outside the store, I slipped on a banana peel, fell and
Watched my nipples clattering down the sidewalk. I could
Hardly move. I had pulled tendons and bruised the ball and
Socket joint in my hip. Someone helped me up and
I limped home with my nipples and water cock."

The teacher looked up and said,
"Does the water heater work now?"

"I milk the sky and the earth."
H. D. Thoreau

That Woodpecker

Outside my office window
this black and white,
red-capped woodpecker
ratta-tat-tatts
ratta-tat-tatts
pecking a bug trail up
the apple tree branch.

Startled, or hungry for more,
or sated perhaps, swish, the
woodpecker flies away,
vanishes before I can say,
"Woodpecker,
when you die,
you will never know it."

Neither will I.

Wooden Fence Post

Tree rings circle the cut face
of this fence post. The rings
SWIRL in a pattern like the
WHORL of my fingerprint.

Tiny frost crystals dot the
CIRCLES with icy stars.

Is this why tree branches
REACH for the heavens?

I look again at the
COSMIC
tree ring
SWIRL;
again the
WHORL
of my fingerprint.

I too reach for the heavens.

Geography 101

Listen up, Jack.
So, you want to define *Places.*
Then how about the Jesuit Novitiate
15 miles west of Reading, P-A, that
pin-head dot of Wernersville,
where I searched for God, Jesus, Nirvana
and falling asleep at morning meditation,
conked my head on the radiator
and swooned among swirling stars.

Places, Jack? Like in the crotched fork in the apple tree
on my farm in Ridgefield, Washington, where I looked up
to a bald eagle with wings as wide as the tree
and in the distance Mount Saint Helens
spewing violent volcanic ash to match Hiroshima.
Another memorable dot on my map.

Places, Jack, dark places, secret places deep within me
where, even against my will I'd want to kill those
who would destroy my children.
Listen up, Jack. Wouldn't you?

Places, Jack.Yes, I know,
you want *Places, a bigger dot.*
How about 28 miles south of Pittsburgh
in Washington, P-A, a.k.a "Little Wushington,"
on West Chestnut street, at Immaculate Conception School
above the belching and black curling soot
rotten-egg sulphurous stench of steel mills, there

in my third grade, that square foot of floor boards
in the coat room, where toothless Sister Remigus
knuckled my temple with her Jesus ring.
Bingo! Blood on the map.

You said, places, Jack, but there's no map dot for
the hairpin turn in Bear Creek Canyon
a mile west of Idledale, Colorado, where
my friend Timothy flew out of his skidding
blue Chevy pickup truck and groaned his last breath,
black night oozing out of his cracked skull.

Enough? Too many places, Jack? Hey,
I know places you don't want to go,
and other places you might despise or envy,
like in the back seat of the rusty Ford in the junkyard
where I tasted the salt of my lover's armpit,
where the square root of two pairs of lips kissing
doubles the circumference of lust,
where I sniffed gun smoke and the
foundry of my dreams forged hard memories.

Jack, you up for more? *Places?*
You know, Jack, every poem has a place:
Dylan Thomas railing at death in front
of a casket; Eliot, sniveling, whimpering in a cafe,
Neruda, barefoot in the sexy surf, gorging himself
with miraculous images from the propellers of the sea.

There are places and then there are *Places*,
Real Places on my map, so infinitesimal you will drive
for days but never encircle them. Yet, how these *Places*
overflow my universe.

Hey, I've hardly begun, Jack. There's the diameter
of places, in the basement at 1388 N. Main street,
like the round rollers on Mom's old Maytag
where my brother Michael elongated his arm
in the longitude and latitude of
crushing rollers sucking him up to his shoulder.
What dot identifies his scream
hanging yet in outer space?

Who can define the Greenwich Mean Time and
GPS map of Faeto, Italy? That exact pinhead of a place
where great grandfather Domenico's sperm
wiggled north, south, east, west and
twitching its tail fertilized the egg
inside my great grandmother Vicenza Prejiuso.

Places, Jack. I know, you want *Places.*
Okay, then let's look at your map.

Quiet of a Spring Morning

I like the quiet of 6:30 a.m.
                              When
The octopus arms of the apple tree,
                              Silently
Tremble with a thousand angelic petals,
                              And
Schools of long sleek white fish
                              Layer
The fairy tale blue sky
                              Which
Blankets down all grasses and dried leaves
                              Under
Watrous waves of air
                              Before
The grapevine's scaly sleeping serpents
                              Stretch
On silver wires. In the distance

The snow on the peaks melts from the top down
To pink granite, pine needle earth slushy snow
Seeping deep to growing moss and other greens
For the belly of the mountain sheep.

Yes, I like the quiet of the morning
                              Even
The dangerous bashing of tectonic plates
                              While
Earth grinds her teeth in her sleep.

Arizona Suaro

With the bravado of a
lonely bandito
the cactus
trigger finger poised
holds up the sky.

Colorado Prairie with the Best of Miles Davis

Driving southward, I look out at the prairie
and see rolling fields of dry
brown toasted grasses, wilting sagebrush,
and turn on, "The Best of Miles Davis."

In the distance, two mesas, flat as tables,
and the gossiping green juniper trees:
I ask, Painter: When you see this land,
how will you interpret, present, paint,
say, the broken blue mussel shells
of that ruffled sky?
The lightly toasted whole wheat
slices of dry hillsides? Or how do you
paint the conversation of the foothills?

So, I ask the Trumpeter:
What saxy riffs will sound out
the rock slide down the slopes?
Drummer: Can you speak for the tumble of
boulders bolting down the ravine?

Oh! Philosopher: You there with the glasses and
tweedy jacket, what to you is this, this hemline of
cedar trees circling the mesa, Being as BEING?

I shouldn't even ask the sculptor, I can already see
steel poles, cardboard sides, marbles for eyes,
shaping into those three antelope munching grasses;

that chubby one, staring at me,
with the eyes of my Uncle Lou's photo.
Here, the Geologist reads the tome of time.
And yes, the Capitalists, survey every inch for streets,
tomorrow's multiple density housing.
So why bother to capture the prairie, just look at
this land and listen to Miles Davis.

Doing Nothing

I have spent seven hours
lying naked in mountain grasses.
Now, in late afternoon
arising to walk
I see my body's print
six feet deep in the grass.
It looks like the yellow grass
you find under dead logs.
Walking away, I keep looking back
to see who is following me.

Coming into Indian Presence
Orme School, at the Indian Kitchen

They spoke to the wind
And the wind heard their vows.
Their hands touched this stream
And water became their face.
Here, the sandy earth heard their footsteps,
A mother her child's breath.

They spoke to their spears
And their spears knew their aim.
Their fingers touched blood
And blood became their race.
Surely, they looked to the heavens
And prayed with their eyes open.

Now, their arrowhead stones,
Mute, fossil fingerprints,
Sleep in the spinal column
Of star-studded deer
Grazing in the night sky.

I Want to Hold Still in the Mountains
For Bobby, Greg, and Tom, R. I. P.

I want to hold still in the mountains.
I want to touch silence in the rocks,
See the sun in the eagle's morning eyes.

I want to hold still in the mountains.

Let the pines grow out of my skin.
Winds howl in my mouth.
Let trout catch me, mule deer stalk me.
Let earth make paths like veins
Through all my grasses.

Hold still in the mountains.

Let the stream drink from my hands.
Stars kneel and pray in my rib cage.
Let the pines warm themselves by my glowing embers.

In the mountains.

Let the snowflakes take communion from my hands.
Moon shine clear through me.
Let the mountains embrace me in their arms.
I need to hold still, in the mountains.

Watching the Hawk Above the Desert
For Jeb Rosebrook

Down past the old Taylor place
Looking for whatever we might find in the
Ancient creek bed, we walked the
Afternoon light up the sheets of red lava rock
Until you looked up to the sky.

The hawk hovered, circling,
And you stood there, looking twice,
Until your eyes took flight
Hovered and circled under the skull
Of wind and sky and peace in your heart.

Up creek you led us to a stone waterfall
Where the pink and red lava rock tumbles
All over itself in a frozen cascading
Of skulls, snake eyes, knees,
A whole body of stone falling
Yet hangs there, like hawk wings.

Farther upstream
You found a wall of rock
Along the creek bed.
You pointed to an ancient
Indian rock picture of a man with
Four arms, like you, Jeb,
Reaching out, two arms to earth
Two wings to sky.

Now, in golden slanting light
This desert prays with open palms
And the rivers and streams of earth and sky
Give us drink from their hands.

I turn to the altar of this land,
Turn to the chalice of this desert valley,
To the communion of snowflake, rock, and raindrop
To ask this for my friend:

"May the sun always rise in
The wings of your heart.
The rain always fall in the
Flower of your hand.
The moon always glisten
In the grains on your ribs.
And the hawk always hover in
The freedom of your dreams."

So be it, my friend.
When the sunlight kneels on your face
And your eyes pray into the wind,
I see you drink from this land
While your wings touch the sky.

Two Haiku
(Haiku are meant to be read twice)

Anti-Bellum

When you sing to me
Rose petals stick to my lips.
I cannot wage war.

Pride

These geese walk on ice.
But when I walk on water
The ice always breaks.

Morning Doves

Dear Myles,

At 6 a.m. the open summer window carries
in the coolest breeze and coo-est cooing from
morning doves on the wires in the alley
the coo-cooing brings the morning to that grace
where bees and hummingbird moths and butterflies
all suckle at the same flowers.

Perhaps you'll be watering new pansy transplants
when from right over head, the coo-cooing
flutes down so you can feel this magical
transparent prayer washing over you.

Looking down from early morning sunfire
you can see these puffy breasted doves
dawdle along the lawn in search of bugs
then see them so closely you can feel
Christ's last supper in the gentleness of their eyes
and St. Augustine's heart in their gentle heads,
soft tuft of scalp feathers, coo-cooing.

The priest at mass said in his homily that
when we protect endangered species
we are performing a sacred act.
Now I know, and you do too, why St. Francis,
compelled by no other reason than their loveliness,
opened their cages and let the doves fly free.

Your friend, Jim

"Tomatoes and Eggplants Ripen at Night"
Giacomo

Redeeming Snowflakes
By an ex-communicant

I am the one who kneels here
in a first-holy-communion white coat.
I am the one pressing together my hands
angel wings, fingertip to fingertip.

I smell the ozone of incense and
fear to look up until I hear the
shifting vestments. At the last second
I am the one who tilts back his head,
eyes to heaven, heart pounding, and
sticks out his tongue to communicate
with falling wafers of pure snow.

I am the shivering one
listening to satanic winds demanding
yes yes yes, and
my guardian angel commanding
no no no.

Yes, now on this winter day,
I am the one here.
I am the one
mouthing melted redemption,
snowflakes whitening my face,
knees, bleeding in the snow.

Grandmother's Bread Song
A variation on the pantoum

On a hill in Italy, Grandmother hums to herself.
Making bread, her memories rise in kneaded dough.
The high pitch voice of a boy calls, "Nonna,
Grandmother! let me help you." And I look into her eyes.

Her dreams rise in the kneaded dough and I ask
To help her carry the loaves to the village oven
Where I look into Grandmother's eyes and see
The loaves baking golden brown. My belly smiles.

I help her carry the loaves from the village oven.
We fold our hands to sit for grace,
I search Grandfather's lips to learn his prayers while
The wine we'll sip shines purple in our glasses.

We fold our hands to say our grace, then
Grandfather soaks the crusty bread in olive oil.
Meatballs steam. The cheese melts. Our faces smile.
The season we sip glows in the purple wine.

Grandmother soaks her bread in pasta sauce.
I wipe my plate clean. Evening bells toll and
The season we sip twinkles in the twilight.
As Grandmother washes our dishes she sings to me.

I wipe my eyes, the dreaming bells fall
Into the sleepy evening. Grandfather corks the wine.
Grandmother washes my face and sings to me.
My dreams, rising in her voice, in my heart.

Sunday Dinner 1956

Uncle Jimmy, here for Sunday dinner,
says the coal miners of Western Pennsylvania
are tunneling right under our house,
right now. So I tilt my head like a robin,
listen, hoping to hear the tap-tapping, chink-
chinking of the Italian and Polish miners' picks.

Mama, tipping lids of steaming pots
wipes her sweaty forehead with her arm
and won't let us help in the kitchen.

In the dining room I set out dishes
printed with a yellow rose: Thump-thump.
Following me, my little sister Barbara Jean,
in a small apron, sets out spoons: Clink-clink.
My brother, Lenny, hauls up the wine jug
from Papa's fruit cellar. My brother, Mike
hand-tests his flat-top haircut.
As soon as we sit around the oval table,
Papa pours small sips of wine into our glasses
but fills his and Mama's and Uncle Jimmy's.

Papa said Grandpa Ciletti, on his first job in America
worked up to his ankles in water in the mines.
Now the arthritis grinds in his knees.
Papa showed me Grandpa's rusty lunch bucket
that creaked when he opened it.

Uncle Jimmy tousles my hair, then
smiles like the banana split in the
ice cream poster in Uncle Dom's drugstore.
Uncle Jimmy crunches celery dipped in
salty peppered olive oil.
He winks at me and points downward
earthward, to remind me of the miners.

If I tap my foot on the rug, in a little beating rhythm,
will the black-faced miners hear me? Will they
look up with a worry to the dark sounds?

Papa, in white shirt and suspenders, tells us
To bow our heads for grace. Always the same,
"Bless us, O Lord,"
With my fingers folded, touching perfectly, tip to tip,
surely Jesus is watching me, blessing us,
and the Italian miners.

We pull apart garlic bread in silver foil,
the air sweet with the steaming slices.
Papa said Grandpa had to eat potato peelings.
Sweet black olives roll across my plate.
My brother Mike kicks me under the table
but we hold back our giggles.
Mama sets down spaghetti crowned with meatballs
and a large platter of my favorite,
oregano roasted chicken just like Grandma Pasqualina's.

Glass to glass we toast wine then
twirl spaghetti onto our forks.
Papa samples a meatball, smiles at my mother then
sprinkles a snowfall of cheese over his pasta.
Uncle Jimmy, napkin under his chin,
pinches bread in his hand and winks again at me.

Face to face at table, the silence in eating while
as we eat, right below us, Western Pennsylvania
Italian coal miners test tap the roof of a seam of coal.
Waiting for biscotti and peaches,
I think of the Italian coal miners
and hope they get to go home for Sunday dinner.

Uncle Joe's Onions

Right after mass and communion on St. Patrick's day, with
big snowflakes fluttering down on him, Uncle Joe's
foot and spade were turning over his garden.
With a sharp stick he furrowed long rows of black earth
then drilled hole after hole and
planted and covered white onion bulbs.

When the rains kept him in, he pulled back the curtain
and in his mind's eye I'm sure he saw the long white
fingers of onions growing deep into the dark earth.
By late April, he knelt on one knee and tugged weeds
from between new green onion stalks.

In early May, knowing the work of sun and rain,
knowing as only Uncle Joe could know, he dug
his shovel deep into the earth to turn out a dozen onions.

First, holding them up to the sun, then tapping off
the dirt, pulling off the first outer skin,
cutting off the hairy roots, and at the spigot,
washing the onions and his hands in cold water.

Up in the kitchen he shook salt over an onion,
bit, then chewed and closed his eyes. Smiling,
he remembered the snowflakes,
and received communion, again.

Chew Mail Pouch

When I grew up in Washington, Pa., a major rite of passage included imitating tough men by filling our mouths with shredded chewing tobacco. Mailpouch was advertised with bold letters on barns: CHEW MAIL POUCH, hence the poem's title and refrain.

CHEW MAIL POUCH

We did, sending Dick Lynch
Into Fisher's store with our 15 cents
As we hid behind mailboxes, and
Anxiously watched him come out.
"Did he get it?"
"I can't see anything in his hands."
"Did you get it?"
"Yep," he grins, and opens his jacket
To the hidden packet of Mail Pouch.

CHEW MAIL POUCH

We did! Imitating the puff-jawed men
Who steered Gallion rollers and road graders.
We jaw-packed the shredded stuff
And knew enough not to swallow
As we perched in Spencer's apple tree
And aimed black spit on ants, because,
Mr. Shivers said, it killed them, instantly.

CHEW MAIL POUCH

I did! To prove I was toughest,
I stuffed my jaw painfully full
Just before the kick-off of our
Patton Panther's Terrace Avenue
Sandlot football game.
My tongue shaped and packed the bitter
Black wad. Yuck! The bitter burning in my mouth.
The spitting, the dribble down my chin.
Oh! The moldy straw barn-board tasting stuff of
Tough men, but how we measured jaw against jaw.

CHEW MAIL POUCH

Yes, I did! And I dry swallowed as the
Ball landed in Bill Bonus's arms and
We charged to smear him and yes,
Yes, his legs hammered into my chest.
I gulped for air and the black tarry
Juices slid down my throat.

CHEW MAIL POUCH

Sick! Instantly sick. I see
Dead ants swimming in my gut.
Sick! All that game, too embarrassed
To spit out the black wad.
Sick! Helped home by teammates.

The road weaving ahead of me, the
Houses bobbing like buoys.
Finally at home, stumbling into the cellar,
Sneaking up to the bathroom,
Hands out, stabilized by walls,
I lean over the toilet to die.
Nothing will come up, nor go down.

CHEW MAIL POUCH

Lying on my stomach
Makes the dizziness worse.
Lying on my back
Puts my stomach in my mouth!
Opening my eyes, the ceiling spins,
Closing my eyes the tiny ants
Are spinning in tobacco juice.

If I slice off a toe, will the
Poison leak out of me?
All of you ants, please! Forgive me.

CHEW MAIL POUCH!
"Treat Yourself To The Very Best"

Oh! The sign-painted barns
Collapsing in my stomach.

Father O'Malley Meets Barbarella
at Her Pinball Machine

Listen up, O'Malley!
You wanted to play with *me*, remember?
So I'm not lighting up, ringing bells
and whistling my whistles while
you just stand there flat footed, breathing hard.

Snap out of it, Dude. Step up and pay your dues,
bring up your balls, pull the hammer,
see the silver orb spinning, smashing my flashing targets
buzzing off my sparkling sparking bumpers.

What's the matter, you getting hot under the collar?
Take it off and go with the flow, O'Malley.
Get a grip, flip my flippers!
Double your bonus points!
Light me up, zing my zingers!

Look at your score—you're heading for a free replay.
Can you handle me twice, O'Malley?
Plunge up another ball, thumb it hard,
loop the loop, shake me, Dude,
flip the flippers, hurry. Snake the shake.
Watch out! Drain ball!

Now the fifth ball. Last chance,
O'Malley. Hey, your fingertips are sweating sweat
against my buttons, you're shaking me, making me so hot
I'm ready to tilt, pass out from vibration vibrations, and
spin into frantic frenetic orbit.

"Yes, yes, yes," Molly Bloom chanted, and
"yes, and yes and yes," and I say "aaaaaaaah,"
roll over your points, jack up the score,
"yes and yes," you're going, K-NOCK,
and "ooooh," you win a free game and I, Barbarella,
am blessed with the pinball wizardry of you, again.
Hardly like saying the Mass, huh, Father O'Malley?
Wanna hear my confession?

House Blessings

Like the dry rooms during a downpour,
warm rooms during the snow storm,
or is it the blue-black hammered thumb
of the Roofer who laid the new shingles?

Water in the pipes? Or the physical conjugation
of copper to copper at the hand of the soldering Plumber?

Gas heat in the stove scorching flesh into
breaded pork chops, or the Roughnecks at
the well-head eating baloney sandwiches and drilling for gas?

House blessings? I prefer this
squeaking oak floor, the door that sticks,
the toilet handle that demands a second shake.
The dust balls convene behind the couch, but
the roof rafters dovetail perfectly,
a billion molecules
held fast by the 16 penny nails
stapling together Douglas fir studs.

Sing the house blessings, the light to
read Shakespeare and pasta recipes,
the hot shower to rinse off ancient granite dust
and ah, the mattress, and fresh-aired pillowcases
and at midnight, yes at midnight
we sigh in sleep and the house dreams.

Grandmother, Grandfather

I slept in my parents, sleeping
in you, sleeping in your parents
and their parents.

Grandmother, like a hand-me-down sweater
I wear your skin, face, eyes, and hold
you so tightly to me.

Grandfather, I remember your plumber's hands;
your loving ears open to anything
I needed to talk about.

I slept in my parents.
I slept in you.
Now you will sleep in me.

I sing my praise to you for
the life and love you give to me
and of all the tangled words in my throat,
Grandmother, Grandfather,
hear me say, I love you
and as daylight turns to darkness
know that you may come to me
and sleep and dream in my arms.

Recipes from Italy

I stay up late at night
to read Italian cookbooks.
I stare at recipes with olives
as if I'll see my great
great grandmother's eyes.

I smell the garlic
to see the white bulbs in
a distant uncle's fingers.
What Italian in me will never
sing an opera?

The bouquet of olive oil,
an aroma from ancient bread ovens,
sun-washed stucco walls,
shadows of pear trees, the fingers
in the air of Italians talking.

Something is missing between my ribs,
in my soul, something far beyond
aromas of pasta sauce, parmesan cheese,
salami. I've lost more than eloquent
words rippled with vowels. I lost more
than Dante's poetry. I lost a genetic
cultural connection with bones and,
blood ancestors who survived the Plague,
planted garlic, built cathedrals. Their
ancient, beautiful faces haunt me in my dreams.

I stay up late to read Italian cookbooks
as if by immersion in their recipes I can
sniff out and track down my soul
and learn to talk with my hands and heart.

I read Italian cookbooks to see
through osso bucco bones, to taste
beyond crunchy biscotti, beyond
mussels in white wine sauce.
Even now I cannot say the word for what is lost.
What it is I search for. So hungrily.
As if cookbooks offer a mystical
exchange, will help me feel my
ancestral blood. Help me feel whole.

That's it! Eureka!
Now I know. I have never
felt *whole*, always been a cultural orphan
relegated to meatballs and spaghetti on Sunday,
parochial schools, and squid on Christmas Eve,
sniffing the aroma of frying peppers,
wondering if we really did come from Italy.

So when my heart is hungry
I stay up late and read
Italian cookbooks and smell the incense
of garlic, prayers, songs, and ancestors in
my grandmother's kitchen.

Italian Omelets

Scramble the eggs in this green bowl
into the whirlpool, clattering fork.
Ah! The aroma of sweet peppers, frying
as they did in my grandfather's kitchen
on a green and wooded hillside
in Faeto, near Foggia, Italy.

Turn up the stove heat until
the peppers sizzle,
fork one out, daub it on a towel.
Your mouth waters.
Taste the Italian sun!

Now the eggs, whipped,
tip the bowl over the skillet
watch the yellow waterfall
crackling into the hot oil sounding
of the ocean in a shell near
the beach along the Adriatic where
my great-great-grandmothers crossed
over from Albania. I hear their voices
in the eggs in their bellies.

Oh, I love to stir the scrambled eggs into the
sweet red and green fried peppers. Watch
them bubble and cook into a fluffy cloud.
"To America," Grandfather Oreste said.
"Me too," said Grandmother Bruno.
"A fritatta," my father, Leonard, said.
"Me too," I say.
"Mangiamo! Let's eat!"

"Beware! The Drums of War"
Big Willy

Holy Faith, White Crosses

Through the screened window we see
this Santa Fe Veterans Cemetery with
white crosses lined up like sewn stitches
on green cloth, machine laid,
rat-a-tat-tat, rat-a-tat-tat.

Trees shade some graves, sunlight illuminates
others.These fossil headstones, mute but
as vocal as the trumpeter's taps at
sundown when even the flag descends
mournfully, trumpet notes falling on
earless crosses, heartless grasses, yes
the flag descends, curled upon itself,
falling on deaf ears in white-boned skulls.

Rat-a-tat-tat;
These trumpet notes, ta-ta-tah, sad verses
of the Catholic mass for the dead
lower the flag into sundown fire-light.
Through the screened window veil
we see the darkening shadows fall
across the graves. We see the darkened minds
of men who start wars but never leave home
to fight them. The evil they beget infects
our prayers and these crosses forever.

The crosses line up: rat a tat tat, rat a tat tat.
Look. Now the flag hangs limp in
the soldier's hand, limp in the hand
in the battlefield trench, limp under the tank tread,
in the caliber of lead bullets, yes, the flag hangs limp.

Through the screened window we cannot face
the dead eye socket to eyeball. Nor hear their
dying whispers, cries for mother, father
lover, brother, sister, God.

Through the screened windows, tiny mesh holes as
faceted as a god's eye, these crosses,
white Xs on a teacher's blackboard,
our lesson for today, forever.
Will we ever learn.

The Wednesday Before Easter

At the crack of dawn, my pulse rushing,
My breath shuddering in the spokes
Of my nightmare, glassy-eyed,
Gasping, I rushed to the living room.
Out the window, above the mountains and Pikes Peak
A full golden-white god's eye of a moon
Pours molten burning light over the hills,
Trees, rooftops: scalding all to silver, brilliant white.
I flinch back, shield my eyes as St. Paul
Before Jesus. The awesome beauty and fire.

But in my mind's eye: a landscape of crushed beets,
Angry baboons screeching, running about,
Killing their brothers, devouring their children,
Desecrating the women, homes, temples.

I call God on 911! No answer. The Pope, out of service.
The Archbishop, "Please select from the menu."
In the sizzling silver moonlight I hear
millions of 911 calls. Millions of cries to Jesus.
But there's no answer. No one home.
Mary's taking Jesus to the orthodontist.

The brilliant white moon, the communion host
Rising in consecration. What good are tears?

I will go outside and hoe a row of dirt. I will
Poke holes in ground soaked with moonlight
And beets. On this Wednesday before Easter,
At the crack of dawn,
I will plant red onions in the red earth.

Black Crows in a Red Sunrise

Quiet.
A pink sky.
Outside my bedroom window
Two crows Caw, Caw, Caw.

The crows fly by, their beady
Orange eyes as tiny
As earth from the moon.

At the corner of Boulder and Tejon streets
The newsstand leaks red with
Morning papers dripping blood news
From the savage hearts of men,
Who arise and do the awful things
Their fathers used to do.

I arise.
Can I do the things
Our fathers used to do?
I cut an orange in half and squeeze
The juice into a glass.
In Bosnia, the women and children bleed.
In Somalia, the children bleed, then sleep, forever.
Hic est enim calix sanguinis mei.
This is *my* blood.

Beneath my skin all is darkness.
What color my heart?
Pink? Red? Purple? Evil?
Would I enter a heart of darkness

To kill. Actually KILL
Those men who rape, pillage, and murder?

The two black crows
Sit on the elm branches.

As I butter burnt toast
The two black crows,
Wings of black toast,
With beady orange eyes,
Stare at me.

I hold up to the now red sunfire
This blackened bread,
Hoc est enim corpus meum,
This is *my* body
And *her* body
And *his* body
And *their* body, and *our* body.

If this were my mother, sister
Daughter, son
Whose blood congeals in the sunfire
Would I enter a savage heart of darkness
And do the things our fathers used to do?

Caw, Caw, CAAAAW.
Do not ask for whom the crows caw
The crows caw for thee.
O Sitting Bull, Sitting Bull
Wherefore art thou now!

De profundus clamavi ad te, O Domini!
Out of the depths I have cried to Thee, O Lord.

CAW CAW CAAAW.
Out of the depths I cry as I arise
To Western Civilization.
I think, I hope, I shall never
Never have to do
The things our fathers. . .

CAW CAAAW CAAAAAAW.
The crows fly with black wings
Like sharp knives slashing
The blood red light of this dawning.
Caw. Caw.
Silence.

At 6 a.m. This Snowy Daylight Dawning

The newspaper photo shows a sled on red snow
in Kosovo, with the caption,
"Shelling kills six children playing in the snow"

When all this world
is white with ice and snow
cold floorboards chill my feet,
the air bites icy cold,
my shoulders hunch up for heat.

I see this life as pure and clean,
the land virgin white, the air Madonna blue,
this moment bright and fairy.
But outside my window
the streetlight turns from green
and now I see upon the snow
red light
RED light
RED LIGHT
From man's own making
red light upon the snow.

Red light tinged with pink.
Red light as gurgling in the lungs.
So where are all our darling children
This day of snow and light?
I fear they lay as bright, as bright
Upon the snow, as this red light.

Kent 4, May 4, 1970

"We were shot today.
Those who were not shot,
Pulled the triggers."

1.
Thousands of buffalo
Were slaughtered today. The
Shoshone, Arapaho, Sioux, and
Blackfoot died again.
This is not a question
Of two boys shot,
Two girls killed.
The Ohio National Guard
Shot and killed four humans beings,
But we all died.

Butterflies have bullet holes in their wings.
Sparrows have nowhere to land.
Deer are not safe to leave tracks.
Eagles have to fly underground.

We have to talk with our ears and eyes.
We were shot today.
Those who were not shot
Pulled the triggers.

Our mouths bulge with bullets.
Our hands are tied behind our backs
And they tell us to pick up bugs with our teeth.
The bullets are in our veins

Passing close to the heart.
Lord, God, Almighty Spirit, whoever You are,
And wherever You are

Since our two brothers and our two sisters
Did not find peace here on earth,
And because they died for peace,
May they find peace in the clouds,
Peace in the rabbits, peace in the raindrops.
May they find peace in the stars.
In sunshine, in the universe.

2.
No young life will spring from their loins.
Death by man is the final death.
The fish are black in the poisoned harbors of Detroit;
The pine trees are choking in Mendocino County;
In New York City babies' lungs
Show up as black ink blots on x-rays;
Strontium-90 lurks with a sword
In mothers' breasts.

This is because Presidents Nixon and Johnson
Read the New Testament twice a day.
This is because the Pentagon and Dow Chemical
Believe in Jesus and follow Gandhi. This is
Because our institutions of higher learning
Have taught Alfie what it's all about.
And the churches have flooded the world
With the doctrine that life is priceless.
Yet, no young life will spring from their loins.
Because our teachers do not lie to us.
Because our politicians tell the truth.

3.
They can shoot us.
But as fast as they fire we will spring up
Like rabbits in the shooting gallery.
They can burn our homes and destroy our fields.
But they cannot touch us, cannot hurt us,
If we love one another.

There is nothing to fear but fear.
This is not a question of four students killed.
The bullets passed through their bodies
And are spinning around the world.
We were shot today; those not shot
Pulled the triggers.

"The Strong Basket Holds Everything"
Pasqualina

Spinning with Galileo

Here in Galileo's cosmos, among planets, moons,
black squirrels chatter in morning mating rites.
In the far pasture a red and white cow drinks
from the creek, lifts and cocks her head,
listens to the calf curled inside of her.
Under the mountain a black bear sleeps with
a clock ticking under her fur.

Here in the cafe we crunch on toast, eat eggs
sunny side up, and swirl milk into coffee.
Eyeing the winter clouds even now
we breathe star dust, gulp sky water.
Picking our teeth, the milky moon
whiting our shoulder, we walk main street,
spinning we spin in a galaxy of swirling stars.

Two More Haiku
(please read them twice)

Reverence

The fence post wears this
White cap of new snow. I too
Stand quiet. Praying.

Abundance

Zucchinis flower,
Grow so many green fruits.
Tonight, lock your doors.

Getting the Newspaper from the Lawn
"I milk the sky and the earth." H. D. Thoreau

I watched this morning's mountain mizzle
Misting dewy drizzle slanting
Windblown rain scud scud scudding
Against windows, across the lawn,
Swirling shower soaking garden greens.

I smelled this morning's fleshy fragrance
Oozing outward from profuse perfumes
Pontificating pompously from resplendent ruby roses.

Oh! Yes! And felt this morning's moisture
As tantalizing tufts of chilly dew-damp
Spears of grass titillated my tip-toeing toes.

I spied this morning's slimy slug's silvery saliva slinking
Up the lettuce leaf where the caped culprit sinfully slurped
Successive succulent sucks of my Saturday salad.

How I tasted this morning's sweet sour saltiness
In the lightly stinging tangy bite
Radiating from a red rocket radish.

Then heard this morning's songbirds chirping
Cheerful choruses, celebrating the biblical end
Of our desiccating deadly drought. Alleluia!

Oh! Yes! Yes! This richness in reading
Heady heart-throbbing headlines
Of this mostly wet and wondrous morning
As I bow, bend, genuflect; then pick up
The soggy news of the world.

Dreaming in Fish Breath
For Jorie Graham

Listen up, Jorie,
evening brings out the fish in me
in the veins of coal under Montana,
where all creatures dream in blue.

Evening brings out the DNA in me,
a tadpole nursing the teats of the moon.
Evening, how easily by dawn
I'll become a frog with green teeth.

Crap. My ticket's already punched.
Seven o'clock wisdom sucks. You can
put more fingernail clippings
into a thimble than you can tweezer
words of wisdom into a gnat's eye.

So kiss my fish lips, Jorie,
And watch me morph into a mermaid.
Love is like Australia.
Truth bubbles in the coffee grounds.
Beauty shines in the fish scales sticking to my face.

Yes, dreaming in blue I can breathe underwater.
Smell the wisdom of my fish breath, Jorie.
Evening brings out the truth in me.

Gorillas in the Mist at the YMCA

That one, him, by the towel rack; him
With his shoulders curving down to
His hairy back to the plump of his butt.
His arms hang forward, dangle loosely,
Not sure where they belong, fingers and
Knuckles curled under. He grunts,
Then moves, step by step, with
Huge and powerful thighs.
Now he lumbers, one plodding step after another,
Into the mist of the steam, the steam into his face,
That flattened nose, bulging brow, heavy chin
Facing into the mist.

All the other men here
With animal angles, curves,
Jutting foreheads, spined sloping,
Buttocks bulging, hairy legs,
Arms dangling, heads rocking back and forth,
As they dry themselves, their animal jaws repeat
Stock market quotes, business deals.
Their watchful eyes in the mist,
Checking out the other's arms, thighs, legs,
Sneaking glances at sexual equipment,
Then their own, to make sure theirs is good enough.
These men in the mist at the YMCA, they grunt, too.

Tangerine

When I am tangerine you will open
my hands, take them to your face,
smell exotic spices, India, Bali.

If I were tangerine my nipples
would have seeds and you
could taste my citrus sweetness
lick my armpits, suck your fingers.

Oh! If I were tangerine the scales
would flake from your eyes and you'd see
the rivers of the world under your fingernails.

But I am not tangerine. So offer up
your hands to my face and let's
both be tangerine.

Ah! The Last Two Haiku

Window Shopping

Knee-deep up river
The fisherman casts his lure.
Catching none, catches all.

Book Lovers Delight

At night the lamp's light
Illuminates these pages,
Lighting up the heart.

In Barney's Diner

Stepping right up, Jack, to the
red white and blue door, push through
to the room of blue smoke, crowded tables,
the fat butts bulging over the counter stools,
tabletops with used plates, empty cups,
driftwood of toast crusts, crumpled napkins.

The waitress, pencil in her hair,
juggles an armload of salad plates to
a table of five in the corner booth:
"Mike," says his Echo Plumbing shirt, lights up,
inhales deeply, sucks in a corner of his lip,
exhales a blue-white wind-sock of smoke.

Mr. Mustache, under his American flag hat,
leans into the corner, arms spread along
the top of the booth; on the window side,
backlit with sunfire, two shadows shovel up lettuce,
while Mr. Crewcut, eating a fistful of bread
pushes aside his salad plate.

"Martha Stewart, using her for a scapegoat."
Gruff voice, " Big-ass box. Told 'im to shove it."
"The more I make the more they take outta my check."
"You can't trust no one nohow."
"The big boys know how to butter their own bread."
The waitress delivers more plates. Mike
hisses out his cigarette in his salad plate.
Steam rises from canned corn, hot gravy,
sliced beef over toast. Smiles. Silence.
Mouths chewing, throats gulping.

Food distracts us from the illusions of
honor, justice, equality, democracy, eternity.
Here, we can push back our suffering
from patented caveman starvation.

Yes, wave on the home-made pie.

Again, top off the coffee.
Turn that toothpick, dude.
Drag on your cigarette, Mike.
America the Beautiful awaits you
in that pipeline pit on the
other side of the red white and blue door.

Peachy

So what's up, Jack? Seen any multiplication tables
in your carrots? Calculus formulas in your salmon filet?
Where do you think ideas come from, Jack?

Listen up, Dude. No man's an island, so sip
the spring water, scramble the eggs,
knead your dreams into fine flour and crusty bread.

Presto! A design for a gas-less car, or
maybe a brighter light bulb, how about settling for a clerk who
can make correct change at the cash register.

Oh! Ye mighty lima beans!
The thrill and power of plump potatoes.
Imagine the inventions in Newton's apples
how they give so generously.

So remember, Jack: eat your broccoli, devour the plums,
taste the luscious tomatoes; a kiss is a kiss until
your ideas blossom and ripen peachy keen.

New Snow, Jack

Hey, Jack, in the infinity of it all,
the shadow belongs to the light, first
this one snowflake on the flagstone,
two flakes, eyelashes, melting, more flakes
now on my face, feel the tingling,
the eyelash touch of snowflakes, and this aroma of
earth and cloud, pregnant with spasms of light,
now in a second a million snowflakes falling,
billions, infinity washing over us,
all shadows disappear,
the dark trees wear white sleeves,
the oval track around the field,
a cosmic ring borrowed from Saturn,
even the shrubs, frosted white
the infinity of snow
white snow
white snow
light
walk this beauty of light
taste the peace in each flake
inhale the spirit, Jack, of star and mystery
most of all, hear the kiss of the hiss of the cosmos
one flake at a time melting on your face.

Always Look Twice

At first you're not sure what you see.
So, squint, look intensely
Into this tree, to the top branch.
See that red-tailed hawk with his
Head turned? Look twice! He's staring at you.

Move slowly and the hawk will
Let you tiptoe closer to
Inspect him until you think
You're close enough
To really see the fire
And mystery
In his eyes.
Then he stands up,
Stretches his wings, and flies
Up and away.

Squint! Look again.
See him rowing his body
Into the blue sky.

Now, lift your arms,
Flap your wings,
Fly after him until you land
In a tree. Now you sit and stare
At someone sneaking up on you.
To see them, always look twice.

When I Die

When I die
Do not sew together my lips
How shall I kiss the wind?
Do not stitch tight my eyelids
How will I see the geese flying,
The shadows left by cut-down pines?

Stop! Don't pour wax into my ears
How will I hear prairie grasses singing?
Bees making honey in my ears?

Don't pump out my blood
Where will my rivers and streams flow?
Trout in me swim?

When I die
Take me to a high mountain
And lay me naked where Shoshone sleep.
Lay me face up with my left hand open
To the sky to catch the rain,
My right hand in earth where my fingertips
Will take root with mushrooms.

Let my eyes remain sprung open
So I can see the eagles coming,
And make sure my head is in tall grass
So green shoots can sprout
Through my ears and hair.

Place an acorn under my back.
Water it. As I lie on that high hill
I will dream of eagles.
When the oak sprouts and lifts me up
The eagles will come.

When you return in a year or so
Do not be afraid.
Simply pick up the eagle feathers there
And toss them into the wind.

Transparent as the Grass

I'd love to be a clump of prairie grass.
Wild grass rising and falling
Lashing the wind with long green whips.

My roots are white
But I grow deep
In dark earth.

Grass.
I want to be simple grass,
Folding arms like clumps of monks,
Or crazy as panicked grass
Throwing arms open to driving rain.

My roots are white
But I grow deep
In dark earth.

I will keep the dead warm and
Lovers will lie around in me,
Cows will chomp on me.
I will become milk
In the swollen breast,
Milk in the baby's mouth.

Fold back the spears.
You can see my heart,
See my roots
Glowing in the dark.

I am transparent as the grass.

In the Sunfire

"Caught by the crabbing sun I walk on fire"
                                    Dylan Thomas

We all walk on fire, breathe fire
see through fire in daily life under the sun.
Morning sun-fire in the kitchen
shines the mirror-glaze of polished wood,
sparkles off the gooseneck faucet.
Yes, the morning blessing of sunfire in the kitchen
where lettuce seedlings lean towards window light
and their tiny cells gobble sun-fire to turn green.
The grain in the wood floor looks up to Saturn, infinity.
The knobs on the stove, stainless steel taillights for
a fire machine going nowhere.

The grapefruit wears a shiny silver beret
and the jam jar lid reflects a silver dollar,
the cellophane bag, a mysterious maze of
folds and creases, valleys, sharp peaks of
glittering shimmering mica schist.

The red soup pot sports a rectangle of
light, the miniature of our window.
Spatulas and spoons in the counter canister
will lift off any second for Mars or Venus.

Sun-fire, tasteless harbinger of all taste.
Odorless, yet smells of every flower it opens.
Soundless, yet what echoes beam from
solar explosions to that seashell in the ear.
And oh! The angles of this light, falling on my hands
spilling into my lap, lighting this page.

Into echoes of fire, I stick out my hands and
warm them in window light, as did
hungry cavemen before me.
The light, the blessing of this light from sunfire,
shining on the floor. I'll walk across
this sunfire all day, and never burn my feet.
We all walk on fire.
Sunfire.